SKAIČIŲ PASAKĖLĖ

THE NUMBER STORY

SMALL BOOK ONE

ENGLISH - LITHUANIAN

Numbers Teach Children
Their Number Names

written and illustrated by

MISS ANNA

Early Reader Edition of *The Number Story 1*
Bronze Medal Winner, 2016 Wishing Shelf Book Award

Library of Congress Control Number: 2018902040

Names: Miss Anna, author.
Title: Number story : numbers teach children their number names / Miss Anna.
Description: Portland, OR: Lumpy Publishing, 2018.
Identifiers: ISBN 978-1-945977-55-8 | LCCN 2018902040
Summary: The pictures and rhymes present stories which introduce numbers 0-10.
Subjects: LCSH Numeration—English--Lithuanian--Pictorial works--Juvenile literature. | BISAC JUVENILE NONFICTION /
Languages: English--Lithuanian
Classification: LCC QA141.3 .M57 2018 | DDC 513—dc23

Publisher: Lumpy Publishing
Website: www.missannabooks.com
Email: missanna@missannabooks.com

Paperback: ISBN 978-1-945977-55-8
Printed in the U.S.A.   2 0 0 5 1 4 2 0

Want to learn our number names?

Nori išmokti skaičių vardus?

It is very easy and a lot of fun!

Tai labai lengva ir smagu!

Say-along our little jingle

Pabandykime kartu!

starting from Number One!

Pradėkime nuo skaičiaus *vienas*!

1

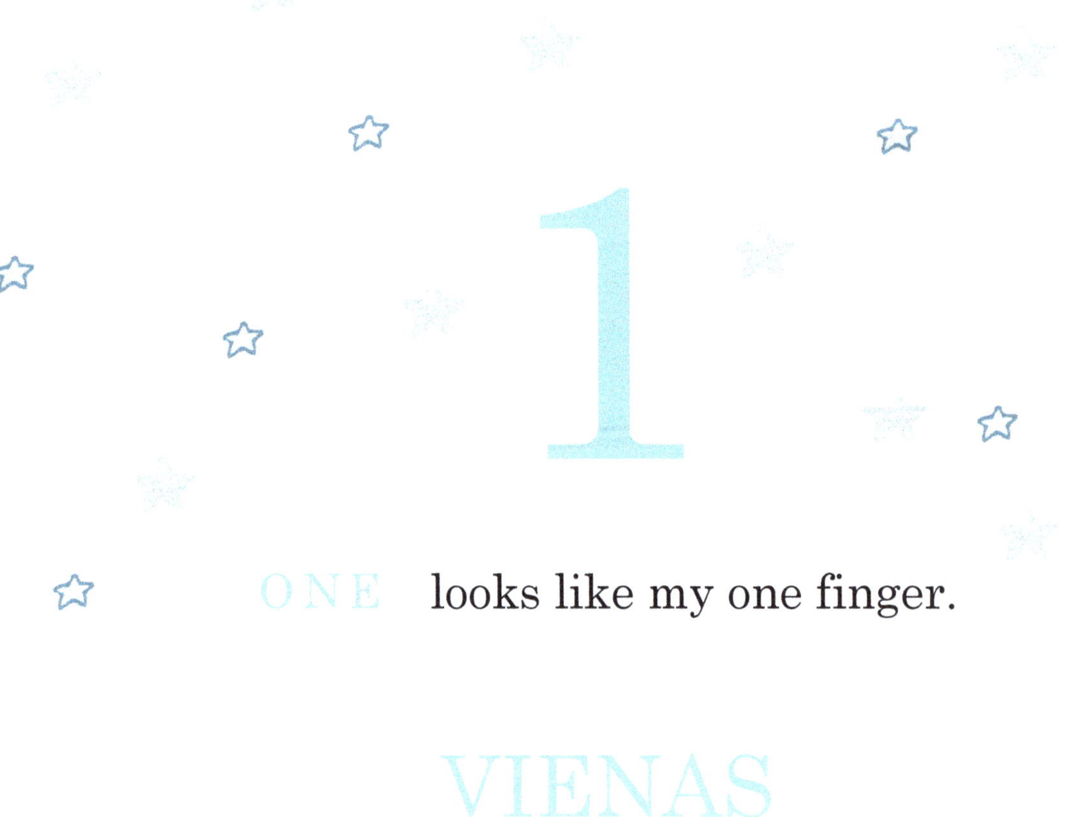

ONE   looks like my one finger.

VIENAS

atrodo kaip pirštas vienas.

ONE!

VIENAS!

2

TWO   trails a tail.

DU

turi uodegą.

A TAIL! UODEGA!

3

THREE has bumps.

TRYS

– su kalniukais.

BUMPY! KALNIUKAI!

4

FOUR carries a sail.

KETURI

turi burę.

4
A SAIL!
BURĖ!

FIVE   is a racing track.

PENKI

– kaip lenktynių trasa.

VROOM
BRUM BRUM!
1

SIX curves like a snail.

ŠEŠI

– riestas, kaip sraigė.

A SNAIL! SRAIGĖ!

7

SEVEN has a sharp angle.

SEPTYNI

turi aštrų kampą.

OUCH!
OI!

8

E I G H T is rollercoaster rails.

AŠTUONI

panašus į linksmuosius kalnelius.

JÈÈÈÈÈÈ!
YIPPEE!

NINE is a bubble on a stick.

– lyg burbulas ant pagaliuko.

A BUBBLE! BURBULAS!

TEN   is an eye of a whale.

DEŠIMT

– kaip viena banginio akis.

HELLO!
LABAS!
WINK!
MIRKT!

And
Ir

0

ZERO is an empty pail.

NULIS

– kaip tuščias kibiras.

IT'S EMPTY!
Jis tuščias!

Thank you for playing with us today.

We had a lot of fun too!

Ačiū, kad šiandien žaidei su mumis.

Mums irgi buvo labai linksma!

We are your Number friends,
Zero to Ten,
Who will be here for you~
Mes – tavo draugai skaičiai:
nuo nulio iki dešimt,
mes visada būsime čia.

Bye-bye now!
See you again soon!
O dabar ate-ate!
Greitai ir vėl susitiksime!

The Numbers are *SINGING* too!

To sing-a-long, look for Miss Anna Number Story
at your favorite music store like iTUNES.

MP3

Numbers 0-10
IDENTIFYING
& COUNTING

Numbers 11-20
& Ordinals
first, second, third...

Numbers 0-100
& Place Values
ones, tens, hundreds...

About Clocks
& Telling Time
hours, minutes, seconds...

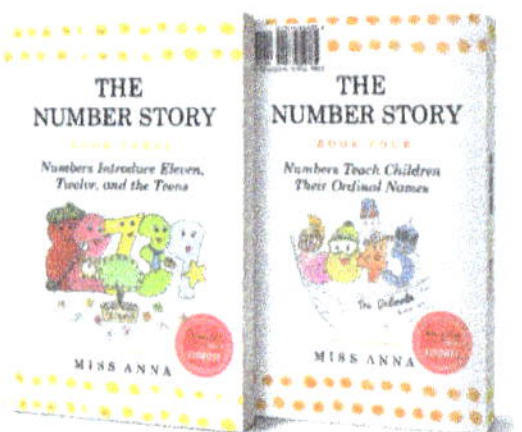

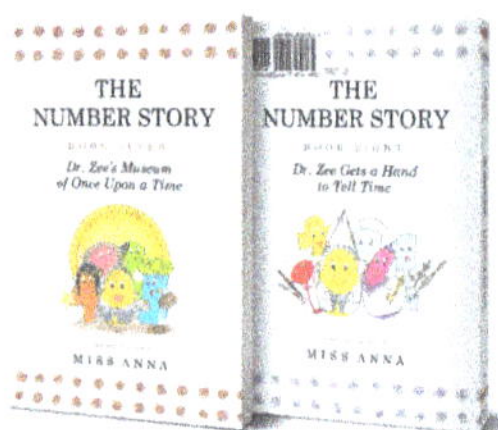

Number Story 1 & 2
isbn: 978-0-996216-48-7

Number Story 3 & 4
isbn: 978-1-945977-01-5

Number Story 5 & 6
isbn: 978-1-945977-06-0

Number Story 7 & 8
isbn: 978-1-949320-40-4

For more Miss Anna books to love,
visit us at

www.missannabooks.com

Numbers are working hard all over the world!
Come Travel the World with Us!